CRISTINA SARALEGUI

A Real-Life Reader Biography

Valerie Menard

Mitchell Lane Publishers, Inc.
P.O. Box 200 • Childs, Maryland 21916

Mitchell Lane
PUBLISHERS

First Printing

Real-Life Reader Biographies

Selena	Robert Rodriguez	Mariah Carey	Rafael Palmeiro
Tommy Nuñez	Trent Dimas	**Cristina Saralegui**	Andres Galarraga
Oscar De La Hoya	Gloria Estefan	Jimmy Smits	Mary Joe Fernandez
Cesar Chavez	Isabel Allende	Vanessa Williams	Sinbad
Bob Vila	Raul Julia	Paula Abdul	Chuck Norris

Library of Congress Cataloging-in-Publication Data
Menard, Valerie.
    Cristina Saralegui / Valerie Menard.
       p. cm. — (A real-life reader biography)
    Summary: A biography of the Cuban American woman who came to the United States at the age of twelve, studied journalism in college, and went on to become the host of a popular Spanish language talk show seen in over eighteen countries.
    ISBN 1-883845-60-2 (lib. bound)
    1. Saralegui, Cristina—Juvenile literature. 2. Television personalities—United States—Biography—Juvenile literature. 3. Hispanic American television personalities—United States—Biography—Juvenile literature. [1. Saralegui, Cristina. 2. Television personalities. 3. Hispanic American television personalities. 4. Cuban Americans—Biography. 5. Women—Biography.] I. Title. II. Series.
PN1992.4.S23M46 1997
791.45′028′092—dc21   97–43427
[B]   CIP
                                                             AC

ABOUT THE AUTHOR: Valerie Menard has been an editor for *Hispanic* magazine since the magazine moved to Austin, Texas, in July, 1994. Before joining the magazine, she was a managing editor of a bilingual weekly, *La Prensa*. Valerie writes from a Latino perspective and as an advocate for Latino causes.

PHOTO CREDITS: cover: courtesy Cristina Saralegui; p. 4 sketch by Barbara Tidman; pp. 9, 10, 12, 14, 15, 20, 22, 23, 24, 26 courtesy Cristina Saralegui.

ACKNOWLEDGMENTS: The following story is an authorized biography. It is based on Valerie Menard's personal interviews with Cristina Saralegui. It has been thoroughly researched, checked for accuracy, and approved for print by Ms. Saralegui. To the best of our knowledge, it represents a true story. Our sincerest appreciation is extended to Cristina Saralegui for her cooperation and for supplying us with personal photographs for this book.

Table of Contents

Chapter 1
A Scary Night

The year was 1960. It seemed like a normal night in Havana, Cuba. But as Francisco Saralegui gathered his family, twelve-year-old Cristina, Francisco's oldest child, knew it would change her life forever. Francisco told his family to pack for a trip. They were leaving Havana that night.

Though her four siblings—Victoria, Francisco Jr., Maria, and Ignacio—thought the family was

In 1960, the Saralegui family left Havana forever.

going on vacation, Cristina stopped to walk outside. She looked at the moon over the sea. She took the time to memorize every sight and smell of her home. "My father only told us we were leaving, not that we were leaving forever," remembers Cristina. "But somehow I knew and I made a point of remembering everything I could to take with me."

That frightened little girl could never dream that she would one day be the host of the most popular, Emmy Award-winning, Spanish-language talk show on television, *El Show de Cristina*.

Today, Cristina Saralegui is the star and creator of *El Show de Cristina*, which is broadcast on the Univision television network. On television in more than eighteen

Cristina took the time to memorize every sight and smell of her home.

countries in Latin America as well as in the United States, 100 million people watch *El Show de Cristina* every day. But Cristina still remembers that scary last night in Havana.

Chapter 2
The Cuban Revolution

> Cristina is also called Mati because one of her brothers couldn't say her name.

Cristina, or Mati, as she's called, was born on January 29, 1948. She received her nickname from one of her brothers, who couldn't say Cristina. He instead called her Matitina, or Mati for short. Before the Cuban revolution, Cristina says her life was like the lives of most kids her age, though maybe a little more strict. She went to a Catholic convent school for girls. It was called *Esclavas del Corazón Sagrado* (Slaves of the

Sacred Heart) and was run by an order of nuns with the same name. "We used to laugh that although the nuns were supposed to be the

Cristina, as a baby, with her mother and father. Taken in Cuba, 1948

Cristina is two years old in this picture.

slaves, in reality we [the students] were," jokes Cristina. But things weren't all bad.

Her education in Cuba, she feels, was great. It prepared her for life in the United States. She became friends with Mrs. Rogers, who had taught her English since the first grade. Mrs. Rogers had a daughter about Cristina's age. She would invite Cristina to her house to play with her little girl, and that was when Cristina learned to speak English well.

In 1959, everything changed. A man named Fidel Castro led a communist revolution [war] and took control of Cuba. His new government would not allow the people to own anything. People's houses and their land were suddenly owned by the government. The Saralegui family had owned a publishing business. Cristina's father knew that it was only a matter of time before the government took his business. He and his family could have been put in prison.

"The telephone companies had already been taken by the government," says Cristina, and for

In 1959, everything changed in Cuba when Fidel Castro took control.

this reason, her father waited until the last minute to prepare the family. "He knew he couldn't tell us in advance because we might tell someone. We couldn't say good-bye to anyone. My father couldn't take any chance that the government would find out and be waiting for us at the airport."

Once the revolution broke out, Cristina's normal childhood came to an end.

Cristina, right, with her mother and sister Victoria

Chapter 3
Life in the United States

The family did arrive safely in the United States. But getting used to life there would take a few years. As Cristina puts it, "We came to Miami [Florida], and getting used to living in the United States was a culture shock like you wouldn't believe." With blond hair and green eyes, Cristina looked like many American girls. But her classmates saw her as different. "They treated us like we were savages," she

The family arrived safely in Miami, Florida.

remembers. "The American kids would come up to me and say, 'Man, your ears are pierced. Do you people pierce your noses too?'"

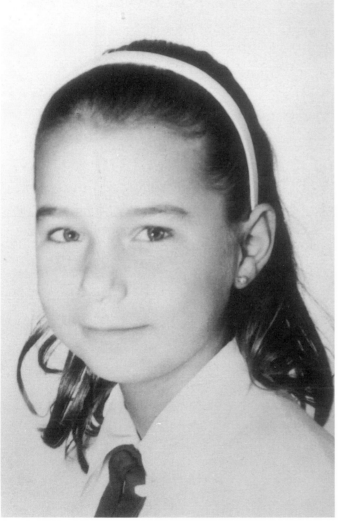

Coming from Cuba, so many things seemed strange to Cristina. As a teenager, she remembers being at a party with her cousins. When they realized that there were boys there and that the parents were gone, they got so scared they stood in a corner and didn't move. "Their parents would drop them off and the kids would dance cheek to cheek. We were terrified. We didn't do that. In Cuba, when you date, you take a brother or a sister or a parent with you."

Cristina at 14 years old. Taken in Miami, Florida

In Cuba, young Latinas are raised to give each other a kiss on the cheek when greeting people. This is a sign of affection. With adults, it is a sign of respect. When Cristina was twelve, she attended a birthday party for one of her school friends. It was her first party in the United States. When she got to the party, she ran and hugged her friend and gave her a kiss on each cheek. The parents looked at her as if she'd suddenly grown another head.

Her favorite subjects in school were English and creative writing. This seems only natural since her parents and grandparents were publishers. It was during these first years in the United States that she began keeping a journal. In her journal, she would write about her feelings and other things she could not talk about. "My family had just arrived [in the U.S.]. They had a lot

Cristina's favorite subjects in school were English and creative writing.

of stress," Cristina explains. "When you leave your country under those circumstances, the kids [wonder], 'Who can I talk to?' I didn't have Mrs. Rogers. [The journal] was all I could trust."

Cristina decided to follow in the family business. She studied journalism at the University of Miami. She took classes for print journalism, but her dream was to become a bilingual journalist who could write in Spanish and English. In her last year in college she had to take an internship, where she studied by working. Her internship was at *Vanidades* magazine. She soon got a full time job there.

Year after year at *Vanidades,* she wrote more and began to edit. *Vanidades* was owned by Editorial America, which publishes several

She studied journalism at the University of Miami.

magazines. In 1973, the company began another magazine, *Cosmopolitan en Español*, and Cristina was hired as a writer. It was the Spanish version of the American magazine *Cosmopolitan*. At *Cosmopolitan* Cristina met editor Helen Gurley Brown. "She taught me a lot about being a working woman," says Cristina. "She shaped my life as a professional woman." Six years later, Cristina became the magazine's editor in chief.

Cristina went to work for *Cosmopolitan en Español*.

Cristina accepted part-time work from other companies while she worked for the magazine. One of her jobs was with the television network Univision. In 1989, the president of the company, Joaquín Blaya, offered her a new job. He said, "I can double your salary with this one job and you can let go of the other six." Her simple response was, "I'm coming." At that moment, the girl who was raised to be a print journalist made the leap into television. She became the host of her own program, *El Show de Cristina*.

Chapter 4
El Show
de Cristina

El Show de Cristina is a daytime talk show like *Oprah*, but it is in Spanish. Because there are few Latino television role models, Cristina is very aware of her responsibility as a television star. She says that she chooses topics that "promote things that are going to help Latinos as a whole." Cristina's show tends to take a respectful tone toward its guests and its audience. Today, she is the producer as well as the host.

El Show de Cristina is a daytime talk show, but it is in Spanish.

Today, Cristina is a popular talk-show host.

One of the topics that Cristina has discussed on her show is illegal immigration. When California

passed Proposition 187, she invited her studio audience to discuss the issue. Proposition 187 denied many services, including an education, to the children of people living in the United States illegally. Many people in Cristina's mostly Cuban-American audience thought that Proposition 187 was a Mexican

Cristina wants her show to be educational as well as entertaining.

problem. Cristina said it could become a Latino problem.

Cristina does not allow a lot of yelling and screaming on her show. She does not think she gets anything accomplished that way.

Another important topic Cristina has talked about is AIDS. Cristina decided to teach Latinos about the disease. "I started studying AIDS among Hispanics," Cristina says. She had three children, and at the time, two of them were teenagers (Cristina Amalia was 19, Stephanie was 15, and Jon was 11). As a mother, Cristina worried about telling younger Latinos about the danger of AIDS. "I realized that the only weapon you can give kids is information."

Cristina prefers to do shows that make her laugh instead of ones that make her cry.

Cristina says that she likes to do shows that make her laugh instead of ones that make her cry, but she's most proud of the shows that deal with serious issues like AIDS. Cristina invited the father of Pedro Zamora, one of the first

Latinos to star on the MTV program *The Real World*, to come on her

Cristina loves children. She often does shows about children.

show. Pedro, who had AIDS, had been a guest on *Cristina* several times. "When we met Pedro Zamora, he represented the young man that all Hispanic mothers and fathers want to have," remembers Cristina. "He was beautiful, strong, respectful, a good student, and a good role model." Pedro's father admitted that he had made a mistake with his children by not talking to them about AIDS.

"I started teaching my own kids [about AIDS]," says Cristina, "and then I started a whole series of shows that was called *Up With Life*." Cristina plans to take her Up With Life campaign on a nationwide tour to help Latinos talk about AIDS.

She started a series of shows called *Up With Life*.

Chapter 5
Future Plans

Cristina wants to pass on her Hispanic heritage to her children.

Full of plans for the future, Cristina doesn't spend much time looking back—although the frightened little Mati is still with her. As a Latina, she believes it's important to pass on her Hispanic heritage to her children. She's told them a lot about Cuba. She's told them what her life there was like, and how life has changed so much for the Cubans who stayed.

"I think every single Cuban-American kid that grows up in the United States has [Cuba] in his mind. As parents, we cannot let that die," Cristina insists. "We have to explain to them where they came from, and even though they're not going back—most of them—you have to always keep your country in your mind." Cristina has no plans to go back, not even to visit. No Saralegui family member is still in Cuba, and her feelings toward the country's dictator, Fidel Castro, and how he changed her life, won't allow her to consider it. "I don't want to go there until Castro leaves . . . or dies."

> She has no plans to go back to Cuba, even to visit.

For now she's happy in her career and with her family. She admits, "The least enjoyable aspect of my career is the lack of privacy and time. It seems like I'm always in a hurry." Cristina has three children. Cristina Amalia is from her first marriage. Stephanie is her stepdaughter. She is the daughter of Cristina's second husband, Marcos Avila, and his first wife. Jon is Cristina and Marcos's son. Marcos Avila was a founding member of the Miami Sound Machine, Gloria and Emilio Estefan's band. Cristina met Avila while she was visiting the Estefans in Peru. They were married on June 9, 1984. According to Cristina, "I met Marcos, and our lives changed forever. Further down the road, when I started my television show, Marcos became my manager, and he handles all the business for our company."

Her future plans include finding more time to write. She copublishes *Cristina La Revista*, a monthly magazine printed in Spanish. Her autobiography, *My*

Life as a Blonde, will be published in 1998 (Warner Books). "My magazine gives me an opportunity to explore in depth many subjects that I can only touch on in television and radio. I want to try to improve the lives of Hispanic Americans to help them become more productive members of their communities."

True to her word, Cristina takes every opportunity to do just that. Whether it's on her show, in her magazine, or on speaking tours, Cristina Saralegui provides her audience, family, and friends with something to think about and to be proud of.

Cristina wants to help improve the lives of Latinos in America.

Chronology

- Born January 29, 1948, Havana, Cuba; mother: Cristina Santamarina; father: Francisco Saralegui
- 1960, family left Cuba in exile, moved to Florida
- Attended the University of Miami to study journalism
- Received internship at *Vanidades* magazine
- 1979, named editor in chief of *Cosmopolitan en Español*
- Married Marcos Avila, June 9, 1984
- 1989, became executive producer of *El Show de Cristina*; six months later, show rated number one in its time slot
- 1990, *El Show de Cristina* won an Emmy Award
- December 1995, honored by the American Foundation for AIDS Research (AmFar) with an award for Distinction for Leadership in Communications and Broadcasting
- 1998, autobiography published by Warner Books

Index